The MAILBOX Songs & Rhymes for Little Learners

Over 80 fun and upbeat ways to build early learning skills

- Listening
- Language development
- Literacy concepts
- Math concepts
- Science concepts

- Fine-motor skills
- Gross-motor skills
- Following directions
- Cooperation
- Self-awareness

Every song and rhyme includes motions or movements.

Managing Editor: Kimberly Brugger-Murphy

Editorial Team: Becky S. Andrews, Diane Badden, Tricia Kylene Brown, Kimberley Bruck, Karen A. Brudnak, Pam Crane, Lynn Drolet, Sarah Foreman, Pierce Foster, Deborah Garmon, Deborah Gibbone, Ada Goren, Tazmen Hansen, Marsha Heim, Lori Z. Henry, Lucia Kemp Henry, Cynthia Holcomb, Debra Liverman, Kitty Lowrance, Jennifer Nunn, Tina Petersen, Mark Rainey, Greg D. Rieves, Hope Rodgers, Rebecca Saunders, Donna K. Teal, Rachael Traylor, Sharon M. Tresino

www.themailbox.com

©2010 The Mailbox® Books
All rights reserved.
ISBN10 #1-56234-939-2 • ISBN13 #978-1-56234-939-4

Table of Contents

What's Inside

Songs and rhymes for **popular themes, seasonal topics, and special days!**

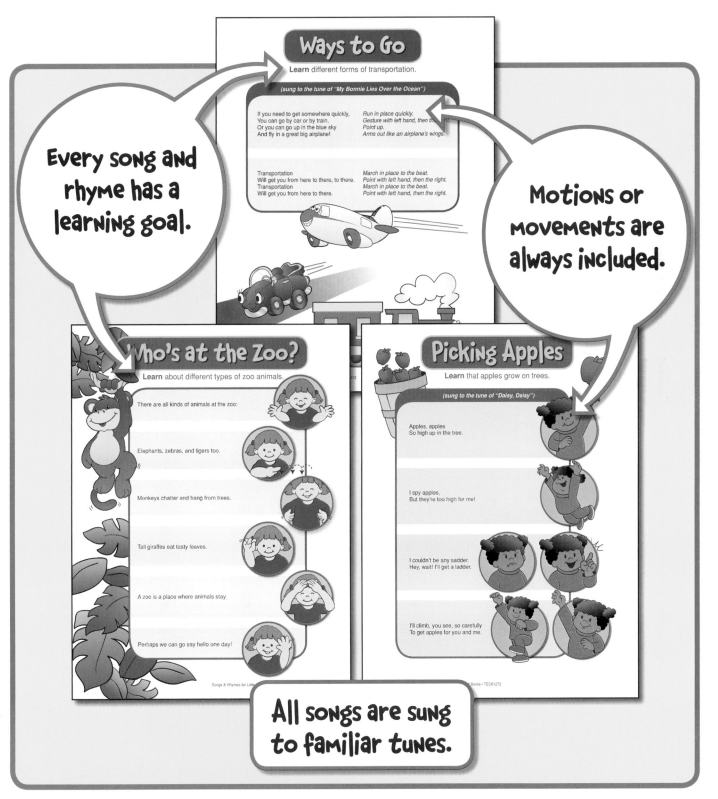

Every song and rhyme has a learning goal.

Ways to Go

Learn different forms of transportation.

(sung to the tune of "My Bonnie Lies Over the Ocean")

If you need to get somewhere quickly,   Run in place quickly.
You can go by car or by train.   Gesture with left hand, then the right.
Or you can go up in the blue sky   Point up.
And fly in a great big airplane!   Arms out like an airplane's wings.

Transportation   March in place to the beat.
Will get you from here to there, to there.   Point with left hand, then the right.
Transportation   March in place to the beat.
Will get you from here to there.   Point with left hand, then the right.

Motions or movements are always included.

Who's at the Zoo?

Learn about different types of zoo animals.

There are all kinds of animals at the zoo:

Elephants, zebras, and tigers too.

Monkeys chatter and hang from trees.

Tall giraffes eat tasty leaves.

A zoo is a place where animals stay.

Perhaps we can go say hello one day!

Songs & Rhymes for Little

Picking Apples

Learn that apples grow on trees.

(sung to the tune of "Daisy, Daisy")

Apples, apples
So high up in the tree.

I spy apples,
But they're too high for me!

I couldn't be any sadder.
Hey, wait! I'll get a ladder.

I'll climb, you see, so carefully
To get apples for you and me.

Books • TEC61272

All songs are sung to familiar tunes.

Home, Sweet Nest

Learn that animals have different homes.

I live in a home
With a roof above my head.

I have a cozy room,
And I sleep in my own bed.

Birds live in nests
Made from leaves and sticks just right.

They tuck their heads beneath their wings
And quietly chirp, "Good night."

Birds of a Feather

Learn about the characteristics of birds.

Most birds fly,
But some don't.

Flap arms like wings.
Shake head "no."

Some birds swim,
But others won't.

Swim with arms.
Shake head "no."

Many birds sing.
Some say words too!

Make a beak with one hand.
Make a beak with the other hand.

Birds are as different
As me and you!

Hands on hips.
Point to self and someone else.

Watch the Birdie!

Learn how birds move.

(sung to the tune of "Jingle Bells")

Birds have wings,
Birds have wings
And feathers everywhere.

You can find one in a tree
Or up in the air.

Birds have wings,
Birds have wings.
Most of them can fly.

Their wings lift them off the ground

And right into the sky.

Can You Fly?

Learn how different types of birds move.

(sung to the tune of "I'm a Little Teapot")

Ostriches are tall, and they can run.	*Stand tall and run in place.*
Penguins dive and swim for fun.	*Pretend to dive and swim.*
Here is something that you might have heard:	*Cup hand at ear to listen.*
They can't fly, but they're still birds!	*Shake pointer finger.*

Birds Lay Eggs

Learn that birds lay eggs.

(sung to the tune of "Row, Row, Row Your Boat")

Birds, birds, birds lay eggs.	*Flap arms like wings.*
They protect them, too,	*Squat down as if sitting on a nest.*
Until their eggs are ready to hatch.	*Jump up.*
That's what birds will do.	*Flap arms like wings.*

Where Is Firefly?

Learn about different types of bugs.

(sung to the tune of "Where Is Thumbkin?")

Where is firefly?
Where is firefly?

There it is!
There it is!

Catch it while you see its light.
Hurry, hurry, it's in sight!

Oops, it's gone.
Oops, it's gone.

Bees Make Honey

Learn about some habits of bees.

(sung to the tune of "Three Blind Mice")

Bees make honey.
Bees make honey.

Yes, they do.
Yes, they do.

They fly to flowers to get what they need.
They make yummy honey each time they succeed.
It's gooey, sticky, and tasty indeed.

Bees make honey.

Hard Workers

Learn about some habits of ants.

(sung to the tune of "Row, Row, Row Your Boat")

Ants, ants, ants at work
In their colony.

Lots of ants with special jobs

Help the family.

How Many Legs?

Learn that insects have six legs.

Insects have six legs. | Hold up six fingers.
They're not like you and me. | Point to legs and shake head left and right.
We each have two legs. | Lift each leg in turn.
They have six, you see. | Get ready to count with both fists up.
1, 2, 3, 4, 5, 6. | Use fingers to count up to six.

Little Caterpillar

Learn about the life cycle of a butterfly.

(sung to the tune of "The Itsy-Bitsy Spider")

The little caterpillar
Ate a bunch of leaves.

It munched and munched and munched
Those leaves 'til it was pleased.

It made a chrysalis,
So warm and safe and dry.

Then one day it came out
As a lovely butterfly.

Everyday Friends

Learn the names of different community helpers.

(sung to the tune of "Are You Sleeping?")

Lots of [teachers],
Lots of [teachers]

Students stand in a circle holding hands, walking left.

Are our friends,
Are our friends.

Students change directions and walk right.

They are here to help us.
They are here to help us

Students walk to the middle of the circle.

Day by day,
Day by day.

Students walk back out to re-form circle.

Continue with the following: *bus drivers, crossing guards, doctors, farmers, firefighters, librarians, mail carriers, nurses, police officers, principals*

The Big Brave Firefighter

Learn how firefighters help the community.

(sung to the tune of "The Itsy-Bitsy Spider")

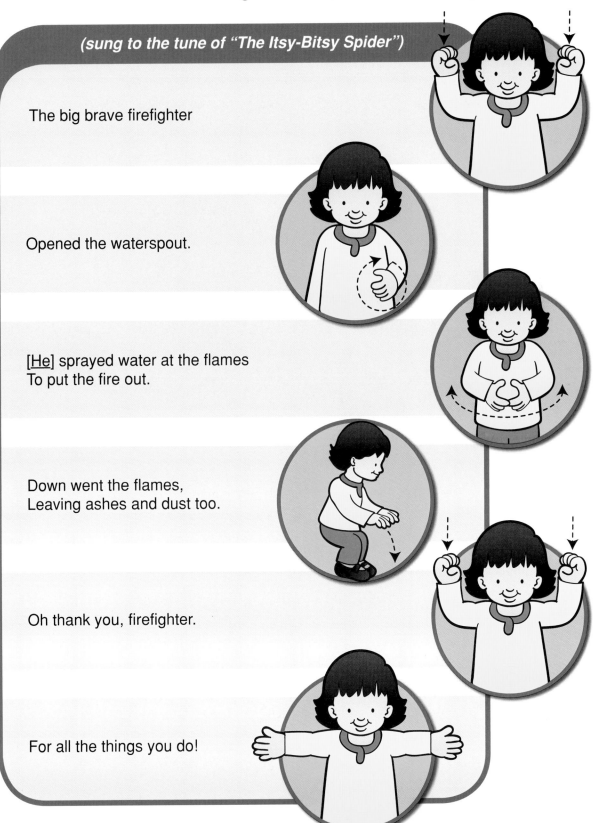

The big brave firefighter

Opened the waterspout.

[He] sprayed water at the flames
To put the fire out.

Down went the flames,
Leaving ashes and dust too.

Oh thank you, firefighter.

For all the things you do!

Special Delivery

Learn how postal workers help the community.

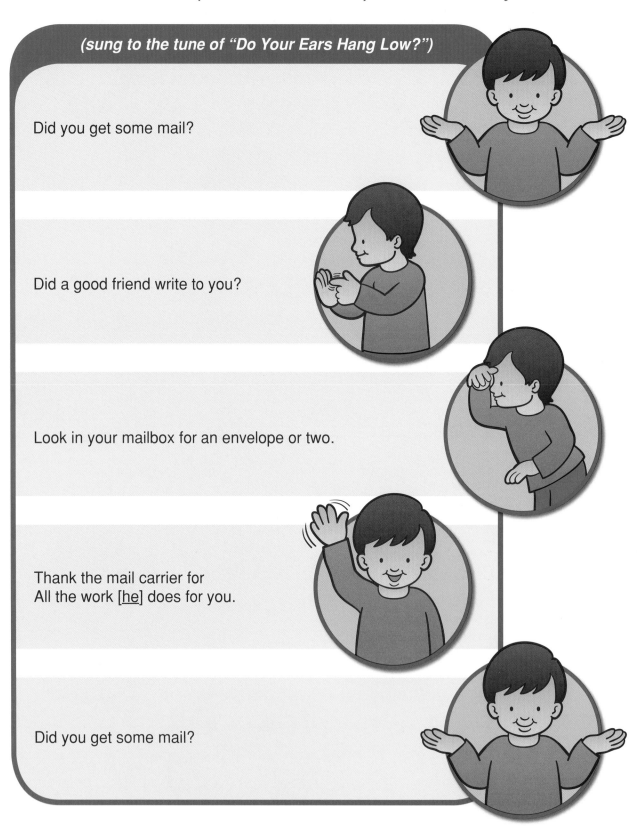

(sung to the tune of "Do Your Ears Hang Low?")

Did you get some mail?

Did a good friend write to you?

Look in your mailbox for an envelope or two.

Thank the mail carrier for
All the work [he] does for you.

Did you get some mail?

People Who Help Us

Learn the names of different community helpers.

(sung to the tune of "She'll Be Comin' Round the Mountain")

We are thankful for the helpers in our lives.
Spoken: [Teachers!]

March in place.
Arms in air; wiggle hands.

We are thankful for the helpers in our lives.
Spoken: [Teachers!]

March in place.
Arms in air; wiggle hands.

We are thankful for the helpers,
We are thankful for the helpers,

March in place.

We are thankful for the helpers in our lives.
Spoken: [Teachers!]

March in place.
Arms in air; wiggle hands.

Continue with the following: *firefighters, police officers, doctors, bus drivers, mail carriers, farmers*

Clapping Dinosaurs

Learn to clap syllables.

One, two, three, four.
Can you clap some dinosaurs?

Hold up fingers as you count.
Clap hands to the beat.

Five, six, seven, eight.
Dinosaurs are really great!

Hold up fingers as you count.
Clap hands to the beat.

Teacher: *Triceratops.*
Student: *Triceratops.*

Adult claps syllables and
child repeats.

Teacher: *Iguanodon.*
Student: *Iguanodon.*

Teacher: *Diplodocus.*
Student: *Diplodocus.*

Teacher: *Pteranodon.*
Student: *Pteranodon.*

Continue the call-and-response portion of the chant
with other dinosaur names, including *Apatosaurus,*
Brachiosaurus, Allosaurus, and *Stegosaurus.*

What's for Dinner?

Learn that some dinosaurs were plant eaters and some were meat eaters.

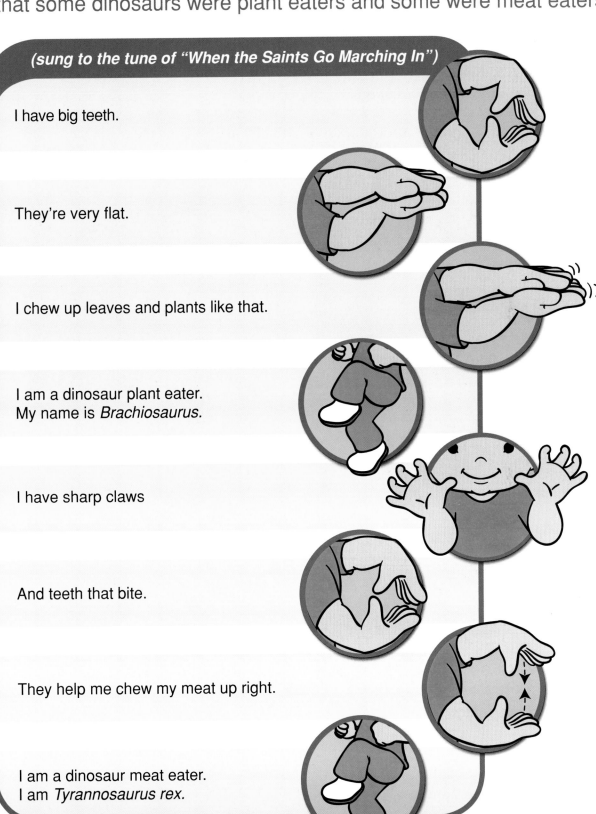

(sung to the tune of "When the Saints Go Marching In")

I have big teeth.

They're very flat.

I chew up leaves and plants like that.

I am a dinosaur plant eater.
My name is *Brachiosaurus.*

I have sharp claws

And teeth that bite.

They help me chew my meat up right.

I am a dinosaur meat eater.
I am *Tyrannosaurus rex.*

Swim, Fly, Stomp

Learn that dinosaurs had different characteristics.

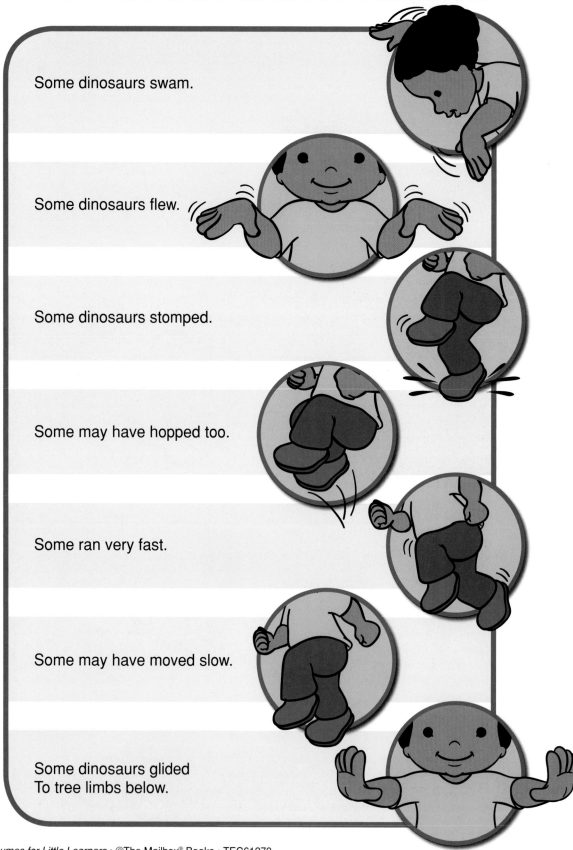

Some dinosaurs swam.

Some dinosaurs flew.

Some dinosaurs stomped.

Some may have hopped too.

Some ran very fast.

Some may have moved slow.

Some dinosaurs glided
To tree limbs below.

Dozens of Dinosaurs

Learn that dinosaurs had different characteristics.

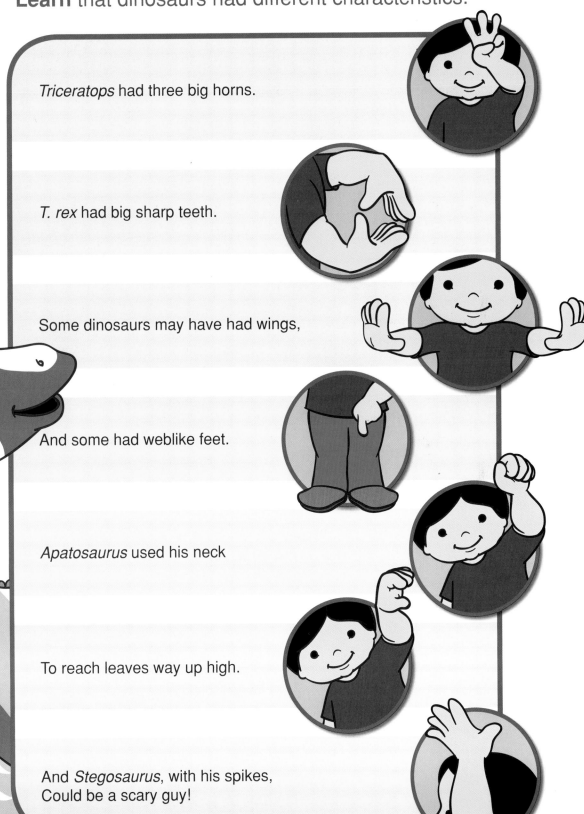

Triceratops had three big horns.

T. rex had big sharp teeth.

Some dinosaurs may have had wings,

And some had weblike feet.

Apatosaurus used his neck

To reach leaves way up high.

And *Stegosaurus*, with his spikes,
Could be a scary guy!

Who's Who?

Learn about the members in a family.

Family, family,
Who makes up a family?

March in a circle with your classmates.

Mothers, fathers, sisters,
  brothers,
Could there be any others?

Face the interior and clap to the beat.

Shrug shoulders.

Grandmas, grandpas, lots
  of cousins,
Uncles, aunties by the dozens.

Clap to the beat.

Lots of folks or just a few.
They are family to you!

Gesture with the left hand and then the right.
Hug yourself.

Sing and Sign

Learn about different kinds of families.

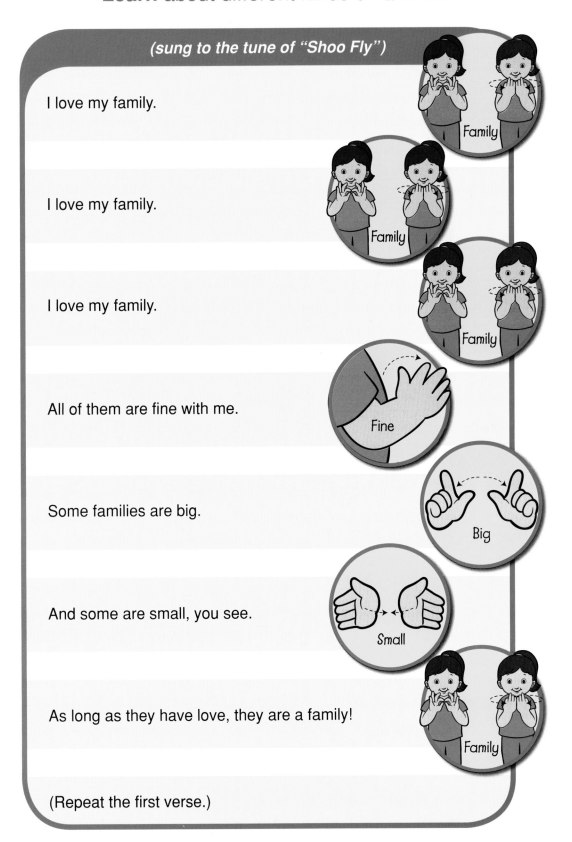

(sung to the tune of "Shoo Fly")

I love my family.

I love my family.

I love my family.

All of them are fine with me.

Some families are big.

And some are small, you see.

As long as they have love, they are a family!

(Repeat the first verse.)

Chore Time

Learn that families share chores.

(sung to the tune of "The Mulberry Bush")

Chorus:
Families all share the work,
Share the work, share the work.
Families all share the work.
We all do our share.

Alternate clapping and patting knees.

It's [mother's] turn to [fix our lunch],

Pretend to stir a bowl.

[Fix our lunch, fix our lunch.]

It's [mother's] turn to [fix our lunch]

When we work together.

(Repeat the chorus between verses.)

Continue with additional verses,
substituting family members and chores.

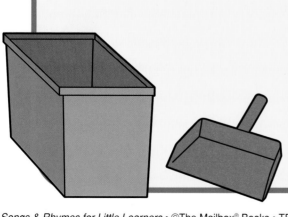

Finger Family

Learn to count to five.

How many people can there be
In my finger family?

Here's the pointer—he's number one.
Find some more to share the fun.

Here's the middle one, number two.
Nice to meet you. How do you do?

Here's the ringer, number three.
Run up high and climb a tree.

Here is the little one, number four.
Bend them down and knock on a door.

Out comes thumb man, number five.
Now my family waves goodbye!

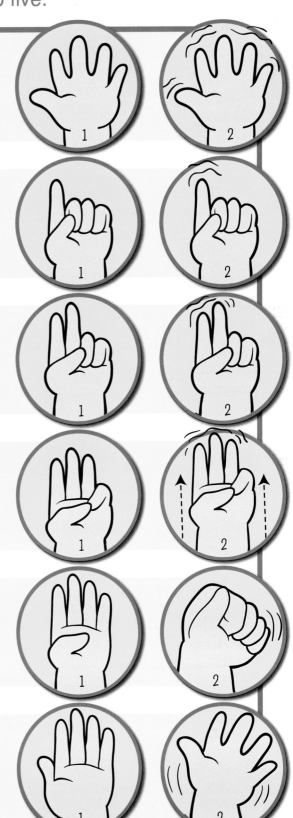

Thank You, Farmer!

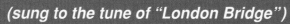

Learn that farmers grow food for us to eat.

(sung to the tune of "London Bridge")

Farmers grow the food we eat,
Food we eat, food we eat.
Farmers grow the food we eat.

Thank you, farmers!

Farm Fun

Learn about jobs on a farm.

(sung to the tune of "The Mulberry Bush")

This is the way we [drive a tractor],
[Drive a tractor, drive a tractor].
This is the way we [drive a tractor]
On our farm today.

Continue with the following: *milk the cows, ride the horse, gather the eggs, pick the pumpkins, shuck the corn, plow the field, feed the hens*

I'm a Dairy Cow

Learn that cows give milk.

(sung to the tune of "I'm a Little Teapot")

Look, a dairy cow all black and white.

It goes to sleep in the barn at night.

When it talks to you,

You hear it moo.

Cows give milk that's good for you.

Moms and Babies

Learn the names of animal babies and their mothers.

The little piglets on the farm belong to the *great* big sow.

The little calves on the farm belong to the *great* big cow.

The little lambs on the farm belong to the *great* big ewe.

And do you know the name for baby goats?

They're kids, just like you!

Farm Animals All Around

Learn the sounds of farm animals.

(sung to the tune of "If You're Happy and You Know It")

On the farm, there is a [horse] that says, "[neigh]!"
On the farm, there is a [horse] that says, "[neigh]!"
Oh that's what a [horse] will do.
It is sure to [neigh] at you!
On the farm, there is a [horse] that says, "[neigh]!"

Galloping

Continue with the following: *cow, moo; hen, cluck; duck, quack; pig, oink; chick, peep*

Moo!

Quack!

Oink!

Cluck!

Five Little Speckled Hens

Learn to count backward from five.

(sung to the tune of "Five Green and Speckled Frogs")

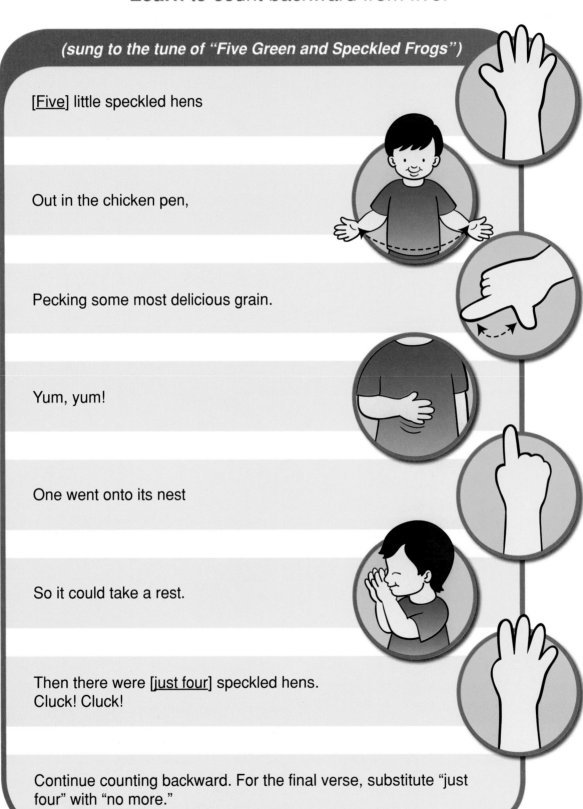

[Five] little speckled hens

Out in the chicken pen,

Pecking some most delicious grain.

Yum, yum!

One went onto its nest

So it could take a rest.

Then there were [just four] speckled hens.
Cluck! Cluck!

Continue counting backward. For the final verse, substitute "just four" with "no more."

Parts of Me

Learn the names of body parts.

I have ten fingers

And ten wiggly toes

But just one tummy

And just one nose.

Two knees,

Two hips,

Two eyes that see—

All these are part of me!

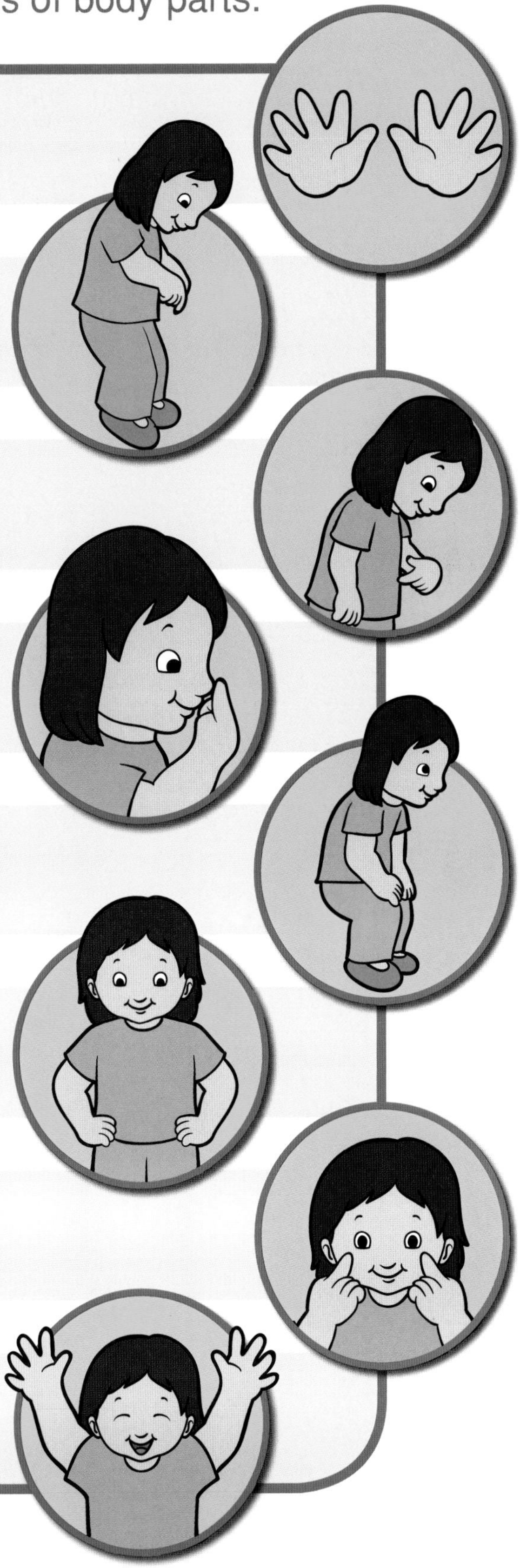

I Have Five Senses

Learn the five senses.

(sung to the tune of "Six Little Ducks")

I use five senses every day

To help me learn

And help me play.

I feel; I hear;

I taste, smell, see.

My five senses are part of me,

Part of me, part of me.

My five senses are part of me!

Sometimes I Feel...

Learn that people experience many feelings.

(sung to the tune of "My Bonnie Lies Over the Ocean")

Oh, sometimes I feel so happy.

Oh, sometimes I feel so sad.

Oh, sometimes I feel so frightened.

And sometimes I feel just plain mad!

Feelings, feelings,
Our feelings can change from time to time.
Feelings, feelings,
Oh, tell me if you feel fine!

I'm Special!

Learn that each person is unique.

(sung to the tune of "He's Got the Whole World in His Hands")

There's no one in the world quite like me!

There's no one in the world quite like me!

There's no one in the world quite like me!

I am as special as can be!

Don't Drink It!

Learn that seawater is salty.

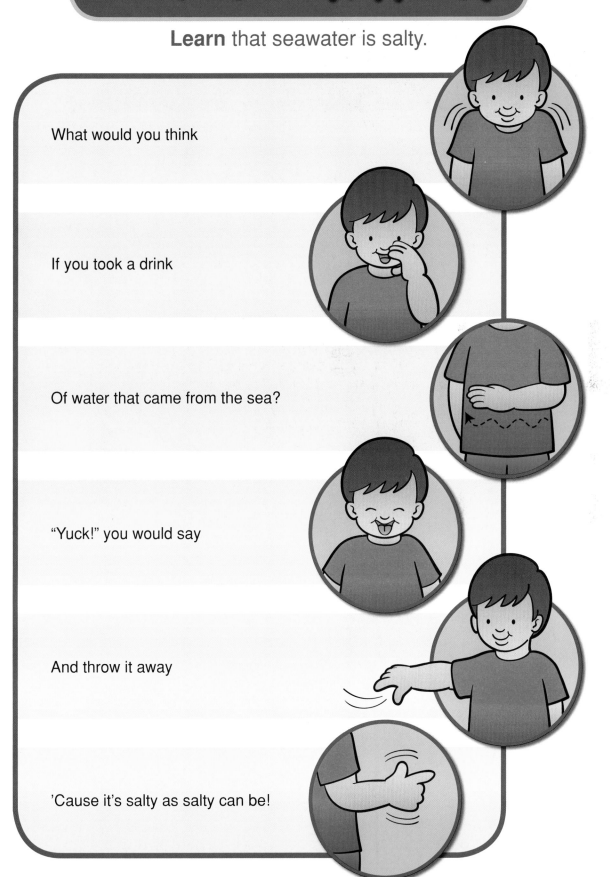

What would you think

If you took a drink

Of water that came from the sea?

"Yuck!" you would say

And throw it away

'Cause it's salty as salty can be!

Ocean Foods

Learn that some foods we eat come from the sea.

(sung to the tune of "Head and Shoulders")

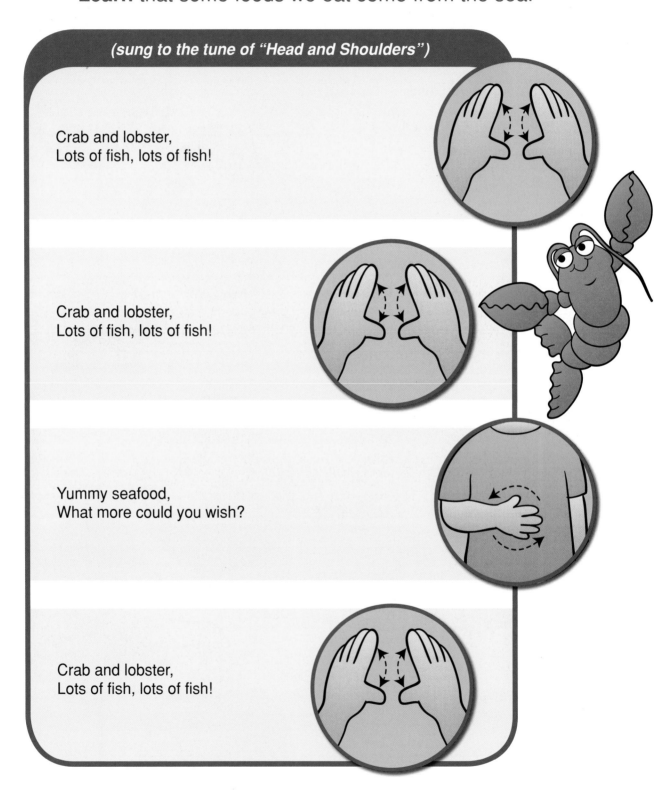

Crab and lobster,
Lots of fish, lots of fish!

Crab and lobster,
Lots of fish, lots of fish!

Yummy seafood,
What more could you wish?

Crab and lobster,
Lots of fish, lots of fish!

Ocean Opposites

Learn words that are opposite.

Dolphins jump high.

Eels swim low.

Little fish dart around to and fro.

The whale is big.

The shrimp is small.

The puffer fish blows up like a ball.

The waves come in.

The waves go out.

That's what the ocean is all about!

Who Am I?

Learn some characteristics of a whale.

(sung to the tune of "I'm a Little Teapot")

I'm a great big mammal
In the sea.
No one is as big as me!
I blow lots of water through my spout.
I'm a whale, without a doubt!

Place hands apart to show big.
Move hand up and down like waves.
Place hands on hips. Shake head no.
Place hands over head like spouting water.
Point to self with thumb.

Beware!

Learn some characteristics of a shark.

(sung to the tune of "I'm a Little Teapot")

A shark keeps swimming day and night.
A shark has quite a toothy bite,

Which gives that shark a sassy grin.
Look out for its dorsal fin!

Swim with arms.
*Make teeth with fingers. Hold out
    arms and chomp fingers together.*
Smile and point to teeth.
*Hold hand on head so it resembles
    a fin.*

Ten Little Seashells

Learn to count to ten.

(sung to the tune of "Ten Little Indians")

One little,

Two little,

Three little seashells.

Four little,

Five little,

Six little seashells.

Seven little,

Eight little,

Nine little seashells.

Ten little shells in the sand!

So Many Pets

Learn that there are many kinds of pets.

(sung to the tune of "Six Little Ducks")

So many pets! Yes, yes, it's true,
Big ones, small ones, tiny ones too.

There are cats and dogs
And fish, I see.

What kind of pet would be the best for me,

Best for me, best for me?

What kind of pet would be the best for me?

Goldfish

Learn about ordinal numbers.

(sung to the tune of the chorus of "Short'nin' Bread")

Want some fishy pets?
Want some goldfish, goldfish?

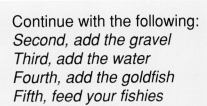

If you want some goldfish,
Here's what you do.

[First, get a fishbowl],
[Fishbowl, fishbowl].

Yes, you [get a fishbowl].
I'm telling you.

Continue with the following:
Second, add the gravel
Third, add the water
Fourth, add the goldfish
Fifth, feed your fishies

Little Kitten

I have a little kitten.
Her fur is soft and gray.

I give my kitten water
And feed her every day.

We go for walks on weekends.
I am so glad we met.

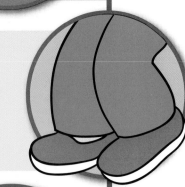

I love my little kitten.
She's a wonderful pet.

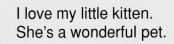

Little Puppies

Learn about actions associated with puppies.

Little puppy dogs run
Zig, zigzag.

Little puppy tails wiggle,
Wag, wag, wag.

Little puppy dogs bark,
"Yip, yip, yap."

Little puppy nails click,
Tap, tap, tap.

Little puppy dogs just
Play, play, play.

Tired little puppies,
What a busy day!

At the Dog Park

Learn to count backward from five.

[Five] big dogs are
Walking in the park,

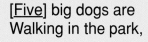

Running with their masters.
Bark, bark, bark!

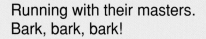

One dog goes home.
It's almost dark.

[Four] big dogs are
Walking in the park.

Continue counting backward until the
second underlined word is *one*.

Fun at the Pond

Learn with positional words that ponds can be used for recreation.

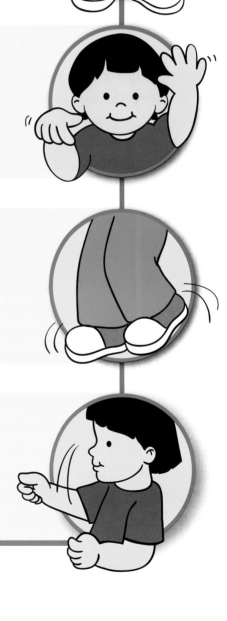

(sung to the tune of "Row, Row, Row Your Boat")

Row, row, row a boat
On the pond so blue.
Rowing, rowing on the pond
Is so fun to do.

Swim, swim, swim around
In the pond so blue.
Swimming, swimming in the pond
Is so fun to do.

Walk, walk, walk awhile
By the pond so blue.
Walking, walking by the pond
Is so fun to do.

Fish, fish, fish awhile
At the pond so blue.
Fishing, fishing at the pond
Is so fun to do.

Talented Beavers

Learn the characteristics of a beaver.

Whose big teeth can chew down trees?

Who can move big branches with ease?

Who can build a dam so strong?

Who works really hard all day long?

Who makes a pond that's nice and deep?

Who goes inside a lodge to sleep?

A beaver!

Little Turtle

Learn that some turtles live in pond environments.

Here's a little turtle.

It has a little shell.

It can live on land

And in water as well.

It walks around so slowly.

Of swimming it is fond.

Where does the little turtle live?

It lives at the pond!

Fish Need Water

Learn that fish need water to survive.

(sung to the tune of "Over in the Meadow")

Over in the meadow
In a pond so blue

Swims a big mama fishy
And her little fishes two.

"Don't leave the water!"
"We won't!" say the two.

[So they stay in the water]
In the pond so blue.

Continue with the following:
Because they need the water
They can't live without water

Ten Little Dragonflies

Learn to count to ten.

(sung to the tune of "Ten Little Indians")

One little, two little, three little dragonflies.
Four little, five little, six little dragonflies.
Seven little, eight little, nine little dragonflies.
Ten dragonflies [by the pond].

Continue with the following: *in the air, on a tree, on a log*

*Hold up the appropriate
number of fingers.*

Wiggle all ten fingers.

Bugs for Lunch!

Learn that frogs eat insects.

Here is a frog sitting on a log

Looking for some bugs to munch, munch, munch.

He eats [one] fly—my, oh my!

That's such a tasty buggy lunch, lunch, lunch.

*Repeat several times, increasing the number each time and having
students hold up the appropriate number of fingers.*

Ways to Go

Learn different forms of transportation.

(sung to the tune of "My Bonnie Lies Over the Ocean")

If you need to get somewhere quickly,
You can go by car or by train.
Or you can go up in the blue sky
And fly in a great big airplane!

Run in place quickly.
Gesture with left hand, then the right.
Point up.
Arms out like an airplane's wings.

Transportation
Will get you from here to there, to there.
Transportation
Will get you from here to there.

March in place to the beat.
Point with left hand, then the right.
March in place to the beat.
Point with left hand, then the right.

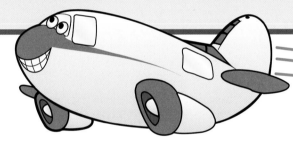

Bike It!

Learn that bicycles are a form of transportation.

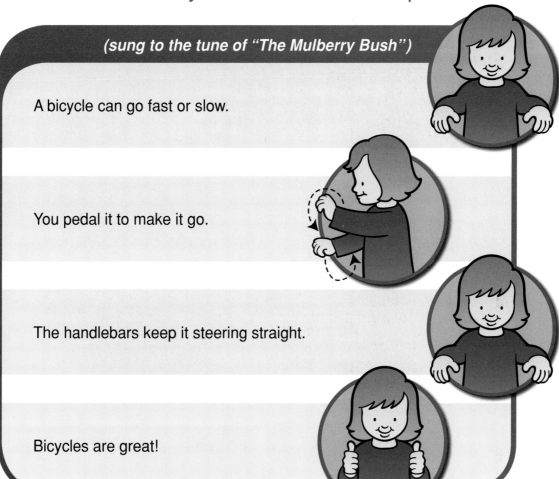

(sung to the tune of "The Mulberry Bush")

A bicycle can go fast or slow.

You pedal it to make it go.

The handlebars keep it steering straight.

Bicycles are great!

Beep, Beep

Learn that cars are a form of transportation.

I have a little motor and	*Point to self.*
Four wheels that take me far.	*Hold up four fingers.*
My horn goes "beep" when I go by.	*Pretend to press the horn.*
Guess what? Yes, I'm a car!	*Pretend to drive a car.*

Up and Away

Learn that planes are a form of transportation.

(sung to the tune of "Do Your Ears Hang Low?")

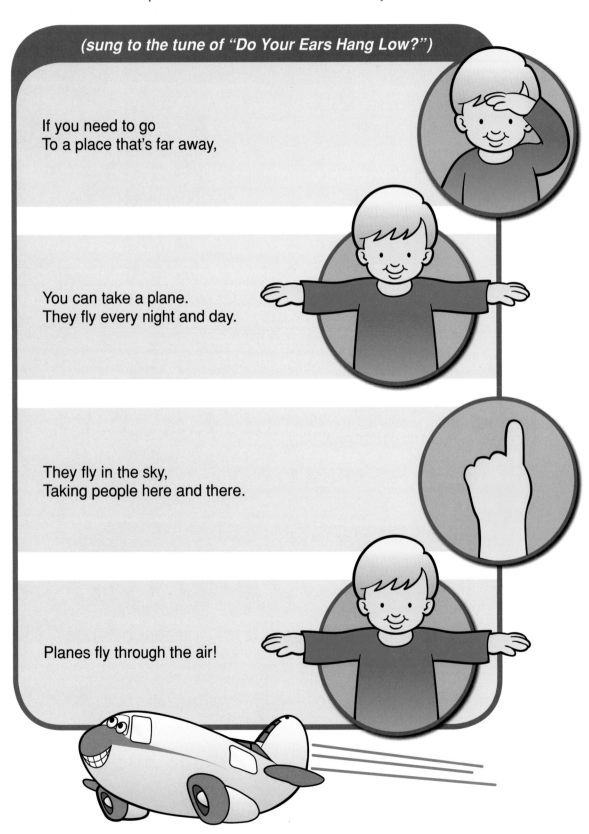

If you need to go
To a place that's far away,

You can take a plane.
They fly every night and day.

They fly in the sky,
Taking people here and there.

Planes fly through the air!

Speeding Through Subways

Learn that subway trains are a form of transportation.

A subway is a place for trains

That go under the ground.

The trains get people on the way

And move them all around.

They can take people to their jobs

And take them shopping too.

These trains will take them quickly.

That's the job subway trains do.

Sail Away

Learn that boats are a form of transportation.

(sung to the tune of "Twinkle, Twinkle, Little Star")

Sailboats floating in the sea,

They're as pretty as can be.

When the wind begins to blow,

All the sailboats start to go.

They begin to move so fast.

We watch them as they sail past.

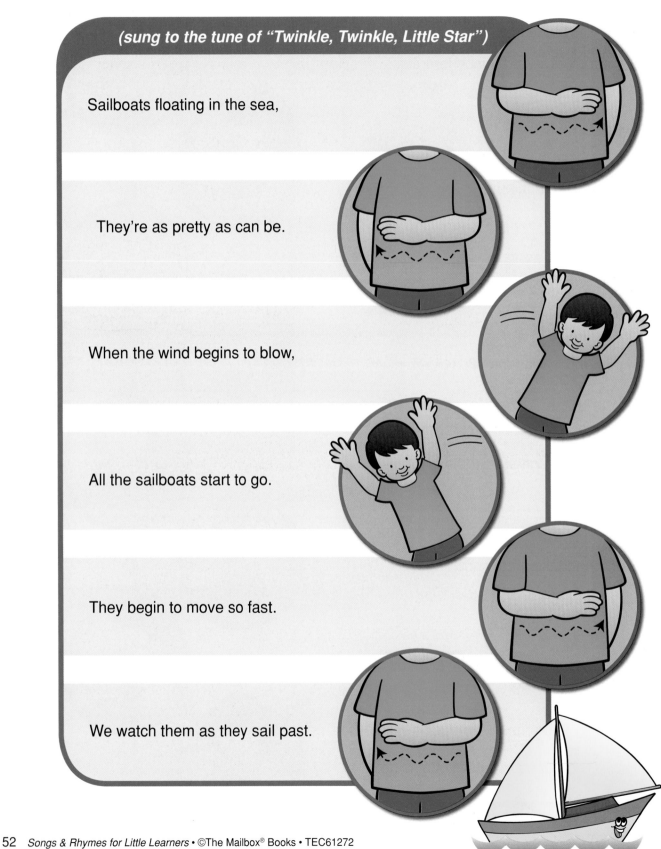

Who's at the Zoo?

Learn about different types of zoo animals.

There are all kinds of animals at the zoo:

Elephants, zebras, and tigers too.

Monkeys chatter and hang from trees.

Tall giraffes eat tasty leaves.

A zoo is a place where animals stay.

Perhaps we can go say hello one day!

Let's Go to the Zoo!

Learn that certain animals live at the zoo.

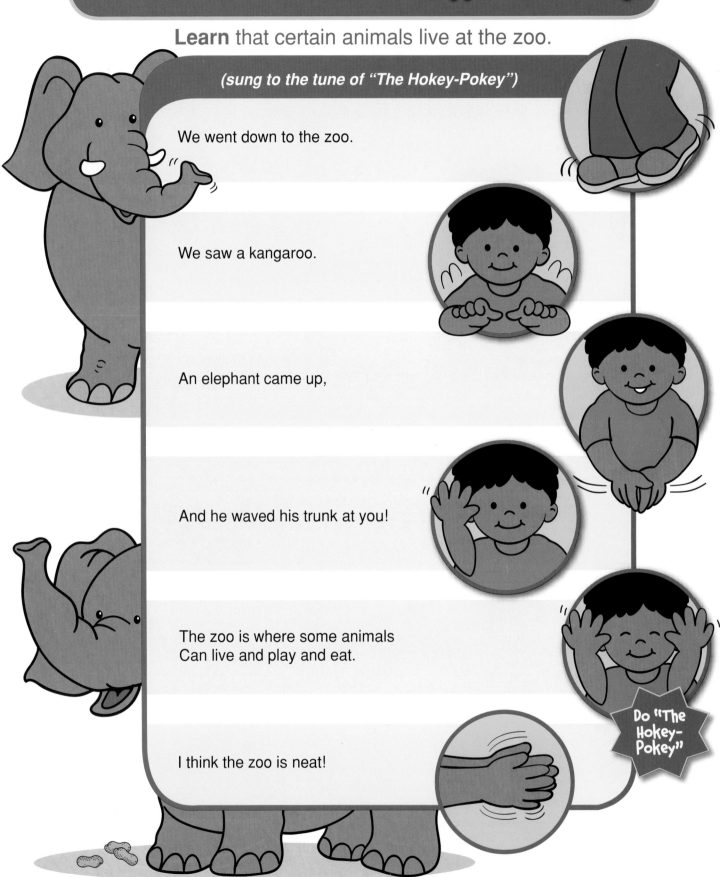

(sung to the tune of "The Hokey-Pokey")

We went down to the zoo.

We saw a kangaroo.

An elephant came up,

And he waved his trunk at you!

The zoo is where some animals
Can live and play and eat.

I think the zoo is neat!

Do "The Hokey-Pokey"

Alphabet Animals

Learn about letter sounds.

G is for gorilla.

F is for fox.

P is for penguins on the rocks.

O is for ocelot, ostrich, and owl.

W is for wolves that howl and howl.

L is for lion and lemur too.

K is for koala and kangaroo.

M is for me, and *Y* is for you.

Let's see animals at the zoo!

Snacktime

Learn what foods some zoo animals eat.

(sung to the tune of "I'm a Little Teapot")

At the zoo the monkeys like to eat

Ripe, sweet bananas for a treat.

Elephants eat hay and

Bears like fish

Or berries for a tasty dish.

Fall Fashion

Learn appropriate clothing choices for fall.

I like fall weather.
There's a nip in the air.

I just put on my [sweater].
I don't care.

When the weather makes me shiver,
I don't mind at all.

I just love the weather
In the fall.

Continue by substituting different pieces of clothing, such as a hat, a jacket, a sweatshirt, or a scarf. Encourage youngsters to create a movement to match each type of clothing.

Picking Apples

Learn that apples grow on trees.

(sung to the tune of "Daisy, Daisy")

Apples, apples
So high up in the tree.

I spy apples,
But they're too high for me!

I couldn't be any sadder.
Hey, wait! I'll get a ladder.

I'll climb, you see, so carefully
To get apples for you and me.

Grandparents Day

Learn about family relationships.

My mom and dad have [mothers]
Who are oh so grand!
They are my [grandmothers]—
The best in all the land.

Pretend to point at mom and dad.
Wave arms in the air.
Place both hands over your heart.
Sweep arm from left to right.

Continue with *fathers* and *grandfathers*.

Leaves All Around!

Learn a characteristic of the fall season.

(sung to the tune of "Mary Had a Little Lamb")

This is how we [rake the leaves],
[Rake the leaves], [rake the leaves].
This is how we [rake the leaves]
All scattered on the ground.

Pretend to rake leaves.

*Move arms parallel to floor
and wiggle fingers.*

Continue with the following and add appropriate motions to each verse:
pile the leaves, jump in the leaves

Ten Red Leaves

Learn presubtraction skills.

[Ten] red leaves are

High on a tree.

One leaf says,
"You can't catch me!"

Off goes the leaf—
Down, down, down. Whee!

[Nine] red leaves are

High on a tree.

Repeat the rhyme until no leaves remain on the tree, altering the words as needed and having students hold up the appropriate number of fingers.

It's Almost Here!

Learn about common Halloween symbols.

(sung to the tune of "The Farmer in the Dell")

I see a [big, black cat].

I see a [big, black cat].

Halloween's near—it's almost here!

I see a [big, black cat].

Continue with the following, substituting the corresponding action for each phrase:

wiggly spider

small, brown bat

yellow moon

Little Squirrel

Learn to count.

I'm a little squirrel
In an old oak tree.

I've got [one acorn],
Yes sirree!

I'll hide [that acorn]
Safely away

To eat for lunch
On a winter day!

Repeat several times, increasing the number of acorns by one each time and having students hold up the correct number of fingers.

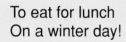

The First Thanksgiving

Learn about the Pilgrims.

On the Mayflower, the Pilgrims came
Many years ago.

They worked hard and planted crops
And helped their crops grow.

When it was time to pick the crops,
They were so very glad

And they said, "Thank you very much!"
For all the food they had.

Santa's Reindeer

Learn ordinal numbers.

Five of Santa's reindeer stood in the snow.	*Hold up five fingers.*
The first one said, "I can't wait to go!"	*Hold up one finger.*
The second one said, "We'll fly so high!"	*Hold up two fingers.*
The third one said, "In the Christmas Eve sky."	*Hold up three fingers.*
The fourth one said, "Santa's on his way."	*Hold up four fingers.*
The fifth one said, "Hip hip hooray!"	*Hold up five fingers.*
"Ho! Ho!" Santa said	*Hold belly like Santa.*
As he hopped into his sleigh.	*Hop.*
Then he and all his reindeer flew up and away!	*Sweep hand out and up.*

Eight Days

Learn Hanukkah traditions.

(sung to the tune of "Mary Had a Little Lamb")

For eight days, we [light the candles],

[Light the candles], [light the candles].
For eight days, we [light the candles].
Hanukkah is here!

Continue with the following: *eat some latkes* and *spin the dreidel.* Invite students to create actions to match each substitution.

Hold up eight fingers and sway.

Clap hands to the beat.

Kwanzaa Colors

Learn the traditional colors of Kwanzaa.

Three colors in my kinara.
Three colors of candles, we light.
Three colors represent Kwanzaa.
Red, black, and green shining bright.

Hold up three fingers.
Touch each finger.
Hold up three fingers.
Wiggle fingers.

Winter Wear

Learn about appropriate winter clothing.

(sung to the tune of "It's Raining, It's Pouring")

It's snowing! It's snowing!

A chilly wind is blowing.

It's cold out there!

My [hat], I'll wear.

Then outdoors I'll be going.

Sing additional verses, replacing the underlined word with different winter clothing options. Have students change their actions to match each new option.

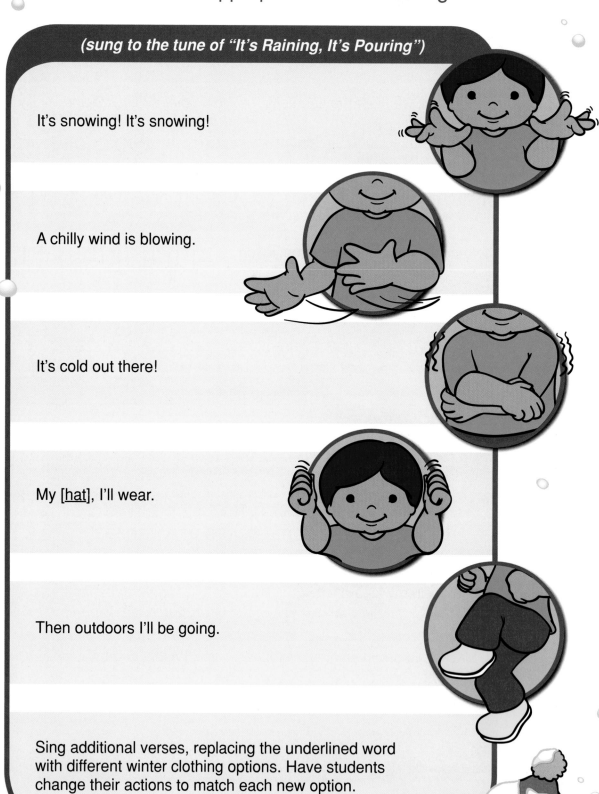

Falling Snow

Learn body parts.

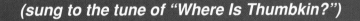

Snow is falling.
Snow is falling.

Cold and white,
Cold and white

Snow falls on my [shoulders].
Snow falls on my [shoulders].

What a sight!
What a sight!

Continue, replacing the underlined body part with the names of other body parts. Have students point to the appropriate body part.

A Jolly Snowpal

Learn about freezing and melting.

(sung to the tune of "I'm a Little Teapot")

I'm a jolly snowpal,
Big and round.

I stand so still and
Don't make a sound.

While it's cold, I'll smile
All night and day.

When it's warm,
I'll melt away!

Hot Cocoa

Learn about a cold weather tradition.

(sung to the tune of "Down by the Bay")

One snowy day,

I thought I'd freeze.

My hands were cold.

I had to sneeze.

I ran inside, and my mother did say,

"Here's cocoa in a cup, so drink it all up.

Chase the chills away!"

Where Is Cupid?

Learn about Valentine's Day symbols.

(sung to the tune of "Where Is Thumbkin?")

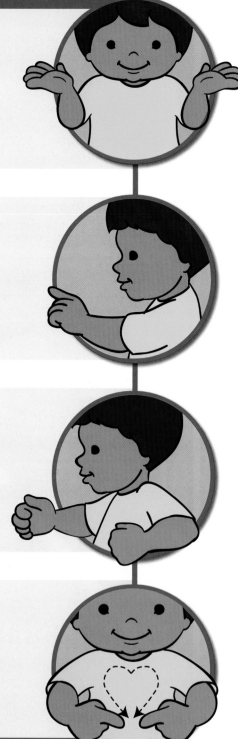

Where is Cupid?
Where is Cupid?

There he is.
There he is.

Watch him shoot his arrow.
Watch him shoot his arrow,

And spread love!
And spread love!

Spring Is Here

Learn characteristics of the spring season.

(sung to the tune of "The Itsy-Bitsy Spider")

Oh, spring comes after winter.

The sun shines all around.

Birds build their nests.

Flowers pop up from the ground.

Springtime means some warm days

And gentle raindrops too.

We know spring's the season

When all things start brand new.

Pot of Gold

Learn symbols of St. Patrick's Day.

(sung to the tune of the chorus of "Jingle Bells")

Pot of gold, pot of gold

At the rainbow's end

Is hidden by a leprechaun

For you to find, my friend.

Pot of gold, pot of gold,

Oh, where can you be?

I think that I just got tricked

By a leprechaun, you see!

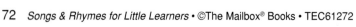

Five Little Kites

Learn ordinal numbers.

Five little kites flew on a windy day.	*Hold up five fingers.*
The first kite said, "Spring is here to stay."	*Hold up one finger and nod.*
The second kite said, "The wind likes to blow."	*Wave two fingers back and forth as kites in the wind.*
The third kite said, "Whoosh! Let's go!"	*Hold three fingers in front of chest and move them upward like a gust of wind.*
The fourth kite said, "Let's fly up high."	*Hold four fingers above head.*
The fifth kite said, "I'll race you to the sky!"	*Hold five fingers in front of chest and move them above head quickly.*

Hello, Easter Bunny

Learn symbols of Easter.

(sung to the tune of "I'm a Little Teapot")

I'm the Easter Bunny.

Look at me!

Ears as long as they can be,

A fluffy little tail, and great big feet—

Soon I'll hop right down your street!

Farm Babies

Learn farm animal sounds.

Down at the farm one day in spring,
All the baby animals begin to sing.

The piglet sings, "Oink!"

The calf sings, "Moo!"

The little baby pigeon sings, "Coo, coo, coo!"

The puppy sings, "Woof!"

The lamb sings, "Baa!"

The little baby goat sings, "Maa, maa, maa!"

The duckling sings, "Quack!"

The chick sings, "Peep!"

At night it's very quiet.
The babies are asleep.

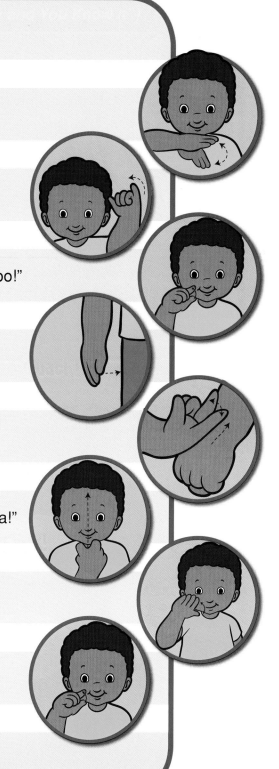

Happy Mother's Day!

Learn to celebrate mothers.

(sung to the tune of "The Hokey-Pokey")

You give your mom a hug.

You give your mom a kiss.

You give your mom a card

And be sure to tell her this:

"Have a happy Mother's Day.

That's what you need to do.

You know that I love you!"

My Summer Garden

Learn common vegetables that grow in a garden.

(sung to the tune of "Six Little Ducks")

My garden has plants in a row. — *Point finger to show several rows.*

I work all summer to help them grow. — *Point to self with thumb.*

I hoe all the weeds, and I water in the heat. — *Pretend to use a hoe and then a hose.*

Then I pick the [carrots]—they're a tasty treat, — *Pretend to pick vegetables.*

Tasty treat, tasty treat! — *Rub tummy.*

I pick the [carrots]—they're a tasty treat!

Repeat several times, substituting other vegetables.

Down at the Pool

Learn to count backward from five.

[Five] little swimmers by the swimming pool.
One dives in—it's time for swimming school!
Splash, splash, splash!
She's keeping cool.
[Four] little swimmers by the swimming pool.

Hold up [five] fingers.
Pretend to dive.
Pretend to splash water.

Hold up [four] fingers.

Final verse:
One little swimmer by the swimming pool.
She dives in—it's time for swimming school!
Splash, splash, splash!
She's keeping cool.
All the little swimmers are in the pool!

Hold up one finger.
Pretend to dive.
Pretend to splash water.

Fling arms outward.

Recite the first stanza. Repeat three more times, reducing the numbers by one each time. Then recite the final verse.

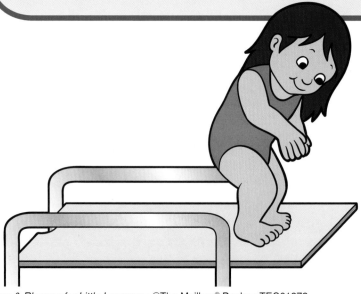

In the Shade

Learn characteristics of summer.

When summer gets too hot for me,

I look for the shade of a leafy tree.

I find a big tree with a shady spot

And relax in the shade where it's cool, not hot!

Super Dads!

Learn to celebrate fathers.

(sung to the tune of "When the Saints Go Marching In")

On Father's Day we cannot wait
To tell our dads we think they're great!
We'll tell our fathers that we love them.
Yes, our dads are all first-rate!

Look at pretend watch on wrist.
Both arms up in the air, hands out.
Both hands on heart.
Two thumbs up.

Pop! Go the Fireworks!

Learn about Independence Day.

(sung to the tune of "Pop! Goes the Weasel")

The Fourth of July is such a fun day.

We swim and eat some hot dogs.

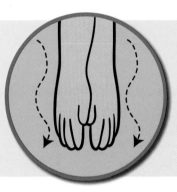

At night we look up at the sky.

"Pop!" go the fireworks!